Letters from Angel

A true story in her own words,

as told to

Martin P. Levin

Skyhorse Publishing

Skyhorse Publishing books may be purchased in bulk at special discounts for sales promotion, corporate gifts, fund-raising, or educational purposes. Special editions can also be created to specifications. For details, contact the Special Sales Department, Skyhorse Publishing, 307 West 36th Street, 11th Floor, New York, NY 10018 or info@skyhorsepublishing.com.

Skyhorse® and Skyhorse Publishing® are registered trademarks of Skyhorse Publishing, Inc.®, a Delaware corporation.

www.skyhorsepublishing.com

10 9 8 7 6 5 4 3 2 1

Library of Congress Cataloging-in-Publication Data is available on file.
ISBN: 978-1-61608-457-8
Printed in China
Cover and illustrations by Mark Parker
Book design by Keira McGuinness

This book is dedicated to

Herminia Paula Drost (Paula)

who made my life a joy forever,

and

to all those who are now mourning or ever mourned a dog.

Letters from Angel

Contents

Letters from Angel

I am writing these letters because it may be
a long time before we see each other again.
I wanted to tell you my story, in my own
way, what happened before we met, our
getting together, and our adventures
But, the most important thing is for
you and Mr. Levin not to worry
—I am really fine now.

{ *a note from me* }

Our first meeting

First I want to thank you for adopting me. That was

a lucky day. I had such a hard time before you came

along, and must have looked terrible the day you

met me. I am a lady, first and foremost, and I like to

look my best at all times. I have been given the gift of a gorgeous coat; it has shades of golden brown tinged with white and black. However, my cage had a dirt floor and no matter how hard I tried to clean my coat by licking my paws and underneath my body, nothing helped. I know my coat was matted and grimy when you found me. I am really sorry about this.

I really also want to apologize for all the noise. It must have been very scary for you and Mr. Levin to walk down the path to my cage with all the loud barking as you went by. It was probably bad manners, but every dog in the shelter wants to find a home so we can share our love and please someone. I hope you understand that every dog you passed wanted to go home with you. To be fair, most other dogs bark more than I do—really loud and long. I am very careful about my bark, and save it for when I think there is a real danger. That is one of the special things about us golden retrievers . . . even if we have a father who was a chow.

When you stopped in front of my cage and my deep brown eyes met yours and I heard you say, "That's our dog," I could hardly believe it. I was thrilled when you crouched down and reached in to pat me. I could tell from your sweet smile, your curly black hair tinged with gray, and how tenderly you held Mr. Levin's hand that you and I would be great friends. It was a magical time for me when the caretaker opened the cage, put my leash on, led me to the walking area, and turned the leash over to you. Frankly, I did not know what to do. If you will recall, I was so nervous that I went over to the nearby tree and started digging. It was a strange move to make, and to this day I do not know why I did this. Your conversation with the shelter manager seemed to take forever, and I couldn't wait for the papers to be signed so I could go home with you. I hope you know how ashamed I am for what happened on the car ride home.

You put me in the back seat of the car and I started to shake uncontrollably. Every part of my body was in spasm. I could hear your words—"good dog," "you will be fine," "we love you"—but I could not stop shaking. Over the years I've thought back and wondered why this happened. I knew that at nine years of age, it was possible no one would ever adopt me and I would spend the rest of my life in a cage with all my love bottled up inside. Was it fear

of the unknown, not knowing where I would be

taken that made me shake? Did you frighten me?

Perhaps I could not figure out what you were going

to do with a very scared and dirty dog. Or was it the recollection that the last time I rode in the back of a car I was taken to the shelter? As we approached my new home I leapt from the car and saw a house surrounded by trees with a lake on one side and what I learned later was the Long Island Sound on the other side. My shaking stopped. There were wide swaths of grass on either side and I promptly peed just to try it out. This looked and felt like a place where a golden retriever mix, namely me, truly belonged. I was then led into a large modern wooden house, two floors, and as I walked up the stairs I saw there were lots of nooks and crannies to explore.

Letters from Angel

What I did not realize was that this was just one of my three new homes. While Rye, New York, was the family house, I would soon discover that there was a winter residence on the beach in Sarasota, Florida, and a swanky apartment in New York City, one block from Central Park, which is sometimes described as a dog paradise. However, I was not ready for what was about to happen to me.

Angel vs. Paula: Round One—Paula Wins

I have had many baths and plenty of grooming by the best in the business since coming to live with you, but nothing compared to that first tumultuous

encounter. As you will recall, you sent Mr. Levin

off to Petco to get food, supplies, and a cage. You

carried me into the pink bathtub and dumped me

unceremoniously into a tub of hot soapy water. I was not a happy camper. Then we began to wrestle. I wanted none of this; you were not to be denied. You scrubbed every part of me. I saw the caked dirt turn the white, frothy water a deep brown. Then as the tub began to empty, even more water started beating down over my head. I'd never had a shower before, and I thought you were trying to drown me. For a moment I wished I was back at the shelter. I was fifty-seven pounds and full of resistance until finally I felt you lift me out of the tub with one arm and a twist of your hip. When I saw that someone as short as you could flip a soaking, struggling dog out of a deep bathtub, I knew I had met my match. But I was not done. If you will recall, with a series of strong shakes I returned a good part of the water, drenching you from head to toe. And you gave me that "I love you but do not do that again" look. I never forgot it.

Our first meal together

When you finally got me dry, you told me it was time to eat. Mr. Levin had returned from shopping with bright and shiny twin dishes and you promptly filled one with water cooled with ice cubes and the other with some food. This was not like my first home or the shelter, and I was confused. I approached the

dishes, sampled the water, and looked around to see if there was another dog close by ready to push me aside and drink the water in my dish instead. No one moved, so I lapped up the water because the long ride and the battle in the bathtub had made me very thirsty. It was great. I never realized how thoughtful it was to serve me the water with ice cubes so it would be cool and refreshing. Looking back, I realize you always did this. It is amazing how a small, caring gesture can make so much difference.

I sniffed the food, rubbed my nose around the dish, looked about, determined that it was all for me, and proceeded to devour it. I had been really hungry. I was not sure what was coming next, but given the excitement of the day, it was time for a nap. When sleeping, I find it important to lay my head across my

forelegs. I looked around for a suitable spot; there were

so many places available. Under a table looked safe.

On a rug looked soft. Aha, I thought, there is a table

with a rug under it—ideal—and so there I went. You

patted me. I felt your soft touch once again. Up to

this time you had tugged and pulled at me. Now, I felt love. Real love for the first time. Really. It was the beginning of our bonding. Water, food, and a lovely long pat, a fine beginning.

Paula vs. Angel: Round Two—Angel Wins

Later that night, I was wakened by footsteps. You and Mr. Levin were turning off the lights and I felt your hand on my thigh, touching gently. You let me shake myself awake. (It's something I do all the time without really knowing it. I just shake my shoulders. It seems to relax my muscles.) I followed you downstairs. Mr. Levin had put the newly purchased

crate alongside your bed. You motioned for me to
go into the crate. Made for large dogs and lined with
a soft carpet, it wasn't so bad even though it was a
small, confined space. Still, I was having none of it.
You held my shanks and urged me in the direction
of the crate, but I refused to be confined when I
had all these wonderful retreats to explore. I looked
around. There was a cool tile floor and fleecy rugs.
Having lived under the stars and subsequently
been penned up in a shelter, what dog in her right
mind would choose a cage with a locked door?
After a while, you finally gave up, and I am forever
grateful to you that you never made me sleep in

the cage (which, as I understand it, is still stored in the garage). And at this time, I would like to thank you for what you ultimately did get for me—a Posturepedic mattress for dogs. It was expensive but worth it, especially for a lady who loves nice things and is just getting ready to enjoy her new life.

*I have always believed
in destiny.*

*I believed that if I gave my love
it would be returned
many times over.*

*As I look at my life, I seldom was able to
choose where to go,
but I always ended up
where I was needed.*

{ **Angel** }

Growing up—and some downs

It is difficult for me to recall my life before we met
. . . it seems so long ago. I do not remember my
mother, except that she was beautiful. Her coat was
even prettier than mine. I never knew my father.

Letters from Angel

(As far as I know, this is true for many humans as well.) My tongue has black streaks, which come from my chow father. I am told I was a cute and happy puppy. I lived with a very nice woman and her three children. She was really very nice and her children loved me. It was fun to play with them. You told me not long ago that you thought the reason I was so gentle with your seventeen-month-old granddaughter, Bela, was that I had been around kids at an early age. This must be true, because when Bela offered me my favorite cracker I took it from her hand gently. I love small children and let them feel my coat. The dark memories that I have come from the father in the family. He was not a very nice man. When I made a mistake, he took a newspaper and whacked me. I had so much to learn. I shudder to think of it, but when he got very angry he took off his belt and hit me so hard that his wife had to stop him.

Not surprisingly, I have always felt more comfortable with women and children. This has been true all my life. I know Mr. Levin, who loved me so much, was always wondering why I drew back when he reached to stroke me. I worked this out with him after we lived together for a while. He walked me a lot. Fed

me scraps from the table. I always felt safe with
him. He was such a loving person that after a while
I changed my ideas about men—especially those
that walk me and feed me treats. But truthfully, I
never got as close to Mr. Levin as I did to you. He

was always understanding when I decided to sleep in your bedroom and not his, even when you were out of town. I did try to make this up to him by visiting his office from time to time, lying quietly under his desk, and letting him pat me. He always had very nice music playing and I loved listening. As with humans, many traits are developed in the early years of a dog's life. I remember my youth, except for the problems I had with the father, as being a very nice time. I got to meet many dogs, but there was no one special. I got along with all the dogs in the neighborhood, except for one male, a black labrador. He was a bully and attacked me. We fought

and I remember he bit the back of my ear, making it bleed. Since that time, as you know, I cannot get along with black labs—and I never will, no matter where they are.

Letters from Angel

Running away

Although there were dark moments, I really did love my growing up. These are the best years for a golden retriever. Still, I was about eight years old and things did not seem to be going well. My family had been changing houses every few years. The father stayed home a lot. He never walked me. He never fed me or played with me. From time to time, for no special reason, he would kick me. One day he really gave me a very bad beating that made me sick to my stomach; when I threw up, he pushed me out into the yard. I felt that I could never go back to that house. We were close to many other houses,

all surrounding a park, and I decided I would try to find another home. I wandered around for several days. I found strengths that I did not know I had. I enjoyed being by myself. My nose led me to the back of houses where I was able to pry open the tops of the garbage cans to get food. There was a running stream nearby and I was able to get water (without ice cubes, unfortunately). People would stop and talk to me, offer their hand, and stroke me. I felt I could live outdoors forever. I found shelter under porches. I found that I loved minty grasses. Rain was a problem, but it was warm and when it stopped I dried out in the sun. After a while many people got

to know me and would leave me some scraps if they found me resting quietly at their back door. There were also some humans who were doing what I was doing—living outside, sleeping on benches in the park. When I got lonely, I would stay close to them. These people loved having me around and often

shared their food with me. Soon everyone thought
that I belonged to the homeless folks. Summer
gave way to fall, a great time of year when the leaves
turned golden autumn colors before falling to the
ground to make a bed for me. Really, this was not a
bad life.

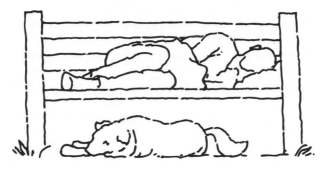

But in a short time it became cold, almost freezing.
Food was harder to find. My friends who also were
homeless sought warmth indoors and I followed
them. This turned out to be a mistake. When my
human friends led me to a hall where they stayed,
a very nice woman looked at my tags and picked up
the telephone. After a while, two men in uniforms
came to pick me up. They put me in a cage in the

back of a truck and took me back to my owners. As they walked me up to the front door, I felt coming home might be a good idea. They talked to the mother and then brought me back to the truck. I was sick to my stomach again. I really loved this

family, except for the man. Why, oh why, would they not let me come back home? You told me later that the woman said her husband would beat me if she let me back in the house. The men took me to the shelter where, six weeks later, we met. You came to see me because my picture was in a newspaper as the "dog of the week." Lucky for me, you found me and brought me home. Thank you.

On a windy day
let's go flying.

There may be no trees
to rest on,

There may be no cloud to ride,

But we will have our wings
and the wind will be with us.

That's enough for me.

{ **Yoko Ono** }

The biggest doghouse in the world

Little did I realize that the next years of my life would be so exciting. It took me weeks to find my way around the house. The ground floor opens out to a large lawn facing an inlet that leads to the Long Island Sound. A dock attached to the land rises and falls by almost fourteen feet as the tides change, and rocks that surround the dock appear at low tide. Our neighbors are a comfortable distance away, but unfortunately they do not have any dogs, so I get very lonely sometimes and have to explore to find friends. As I saw when I was brought home there is a lawn in front and a driveway that leads to the two-lane street called

Letters from Angel

Kirby Lane. If people come to visit, as the mailman does almost every day (we get along fine, since he always gives me a treat) they drive up to the house. There are three ways for guests to enter: through the garage (which opens with a clicker), through the front door, or through large glass doors around back (if there is someone to open them). Really, there are four ways to enter, as a path alongside the rock garden leads to the back door of the kitchen. Going from a cage with one locked door to a big house with four doors is very confusing. I am reasonably smart, but it took me a long time to get a handle on the situation.

Letters from Angel

Paula, I think both you and Mr. Levin decided that it would be great if I were given the run of the house, and therefore since we had all this land he would install an invisible fence. I would wear a collar that would receive an electrical current should I go beyond the unseen boundary. The idea appeared to make both of you happy. I am a smart dog and would, in time, know when I passed beyond the invisible fence. I would live freely and happily in the biggest doghouse in the world. Like the crate, the fence turned out to be a well-meant but useless idea. Once you saw me get zapped and looked into my eyes, you turned off the fence. The collar sits unused along with the crate in the garage.

Our daily schedule in Rye – walk, meet friend and foe

The book you read on golden retrievers said that

they needed to be walked regularly. Since you, Paula,

are the early riser, you take me for my morning

walks. I like to trot, especially at the beginning,
and you are pretty good at keeping up with me.
I understand that the books say the human is
supposed to go first. I let you do this sometimes to
make you feel like an alpha woman. Our regular
walks start along a road that is often busy but is fairly
safe in the early morning. We follow the shore of a
lake and then we swing by the country club, past the
bird park (with its big NO DOGS ALLOWED sign), then
across a bridge over another lake and up a steep
hill to where those terrible black labs live. Then a
turn to the right, past a traffic light, down the hill
to Kirby Lane, up and down a small hill, around a

wiggly patch in the road where you can see more water on the left, and finally home. You have told me the route is 2.2 miles. Not bad, but I understand you walk or run this loop three times a day when you are really upset.

When Mr. Levin is home or it is the weekend, he takes me about half as far in the morning, turning around before we reach the bridge. Often, one of you takes me on a second short walk, sometimes down a woodsy path to the water for a look (or a dip on a hot day), then back through the nearby marina, and along the path home where the rabbits and the

groundhogs live. I am happy to take either route,

especially if I get three walks a day, not counting the

brief outing before your bedtime to let me answer

nature's call.

Letters from Angel

Mr. Levin often goes to his office in New York City so we take him in the car to the train. I am able, on command, to jump into the back seat. When you roll the right window down, I poke my head through the opening so that the breeze makes my ears stand up. I never bark at the dogs I see walking because I say, "Look at me, I am riding and there you are walking. How about that? Pretty nifty for a dog who was just adopted from a shelter." When Mr. Levin

comes back from the city, we meet him at the train. I sit in my usual place with my head poked out of the window until I see or smell him. I try to conceal just how happy I am to see him. It is not appropriate, I think, to show emotions in public. I do let Mr. Levin take me for a walk when he comes home so he knows I love his company; he shows his appreciation by giving me treats.

What I have never been able to figure out is why Mr. Levin's pockets are always full of treats and yours are not. Not that I need the treats to survive. I am well fed, three times a day. Treats let me know I did something right or that you enjoy my company. I am really here to protect you when needed. Let me tell you how important treats can be. For a long time whenever I walked with either of you and I met a new dog, I would sniff around. If I felt you tighten the leash or if the other dog started toward you, I would bark, and sometimes show my teeth in anger because I thought the other dog would harm you. Mr. Levin started to calm me down when he saw a new dog by being relaxed and then offering me a treat so that I could comfortably do my exploration. It took some time for me to get the idea that this meant there was no need for anger. But over the years, with the help of treats, I became a very friendly dog—except to black labs, of course. I still hate them.

As time went by, I developed many close friends. Whenever I saw Flash and Scarlet (dog friends living down the road), you would take me off the leash and we would all walk together. For the record, let me say categorically that I love all small dogs. They can do no wrong in my book.

Letters from Angel

Fit to fly

White coats scare me, so when you took me to the
veterinarian I was worried. What I did not know was
that when December came I would be expected to
go with you and Mr. Levin to Sarasota, Florida. Not
that this was bad, but I learned we would be taking
an airplane to get there—and I had never been on
an airplane. I was told that all the training I had
to take to become certified as a "service dog" was
so I could fly in the cabin with you and Mr. Levin.
The reason for this visit was to see if I was healthy
enough to fly in the main cabin of the airplane.
Fortunately, or maybe not so fortunately, the vet said

Letters from Angel

I was in good health and I was "fit to fly." He gave you some little white pills for the flight. I am not a big fan of taking medicine, but I agreed it would be a good idea to have them handy just in case I needed something to calm me down.

The day came for us to go and I sat in the back of the shiny black limo that took us to JFK airport.

The trip started badly. The driver would not open the window so I could put my head out because he was going to drive very fast. When we got to the airport, it took a long time to sort out what bags to check and what bags we needed to take on the

airplane. It was a hassle. When we started on our
way to the gate, I really had to pee—so I did. (I am
always embarrassed when I do this in public; I try so
hard to please.) I felt better, but you were not very
happy wiping up my mess with a towel.

After some time, we got on the airplane and I found
my seat in between you and Mr. Levin. I knew I was
much heavier than when I first was adopted. The
food you cooked for me was excellent and made up
for all the meals I scrounged from the garbage. At
this time, I was about eighty pounds, give or take a
little. The airline wanted me to be lying down on

takeoff, but there really was not much room for me.
When I felt the plane rising from the runway my
heart sank. I have never felt a pull like this. I was
scared half to death and I started to shake.

You tried to calm me. Mr. Levin reached down and
offered me a treat and I thought, "Not now, Mr.
Levin, please." It took a little while for the airplane
to level off and every sensory organ of my body
told me that I was in great trouble. I continued to
shake. I tried to get up on the seat but it was too
slippery for me. I twisted my body in an attempt to
steady myself and this did not work. My shaking got

worse. I could feel the anguish in your touch; you saw me frightened and out of control. You reached down, put a little pill in my mouth, and held my jaws closed until I swallowed. It helped a little but I was still shaking. You talked with Mr. Levin then gave me another pill. I was so glad to get it that I held

still until it slipped into my stomach. I felt a little better but was still shaking. The third pill proved the charm, and finally I felt my body relax. The shaking stopped, and I had the best dream any dog has ever had. I was free, a young golden running with a pack of other goldens across green fields and down to the water, and swimming, swimming, swimming, until I heard a voice saying, "Angel, wake up." I felt some water on my face and barely opened an eye. A man in uniform said, "We have to turn this airplane in a half hour and we cannot let your dog sleep any longer." I felt your sturdy arms around my middle and remember you carrying me off the airplane and putting me in a wheelchair. Mr. Levin trailed behind us carrying all the bags. It seems I failed my first assignment as a service dog to Mr. Levin.

I cannot really remember anything that happened after the flight, but you said that while wheeling me, I was slipping drunkenly from side to side. The people in the airport laughed at the sight of a struggling golden retriever being wheeled by a lady followed by an old guy carrying their bags. This did not end the episode because you had to flip me once more, into the back seat of a car so we could drive about fifty miles to the apartment in Sarasota.

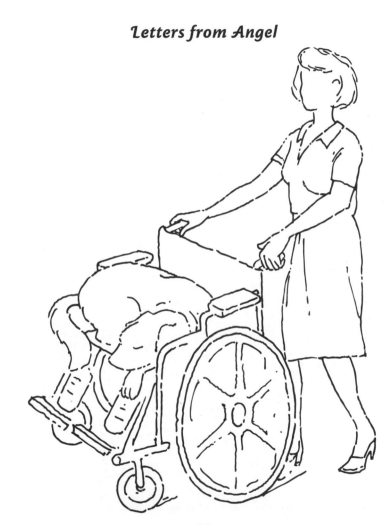

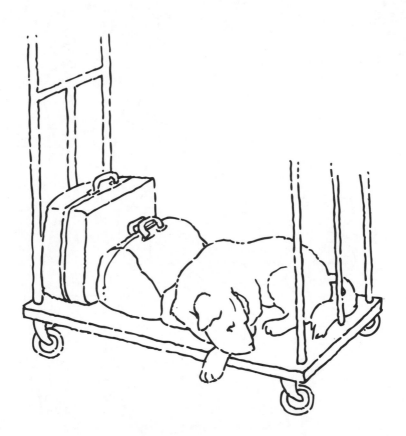

Letters from Angel

You said that before going to the apartment we stopped at Pet Mart and had a vet examine me, and he said I was fine and that all I needed was sleep. When I got to Sarasota, I had to be put on a luggage cart and wheeled on to the elevator to get to our apartment on the sixth floor. It was just our luck to have a cluster of neighbors sitting outside, and they broke up in laughter and applause as I was wheeled inside. What I do remember clearly was waking Mr. Levin at two in the morning and him taking me, still wobbling in a drunken fashion, down to the elevator. After restraining myself for the ride I lunged out into the parking lot and had a world-class pee that made me feel much better. Afterward, I turned around, went back upstairs, woke up early, and had a great time walking along the beach on Siesta Key for the first time with Mr. Levin. What a dramatic way to make an entrance.

*It's a beautiful day
in the neighborhood
A beautiful day for
your neighbor*

*Would you be mine?
Could you be mine?*

*I have always wanted to have
a neighbor like you...*

So let's make this a beautiful day.

Mr. Rogers

New challenges and a new friend

When my body finally got rid of all the in-flight

medicine, I looked around the Sarasota apartment,

which is really two apartments next to each other. One

is Mr. Levin's office and he sleeps there; the other

is for Mr. Levin's family, who usually come down to

Sarasota at Christmas time and on other holidays. I am

happy that you are now staying at the other apartment.

Compared to the house in Rye, it is tiny. There are two

bedrooms, a kitchen, and two bathrooms, but what

I really like is the patio facing the Gulf of Mexico. It

certainly has more room than the shelter, and is far

more comfortable. There are nice, deep carpets on

most of the floors and my food trays are nearby in the kitchen, so that works out fine. You were also very nice to get me another Posturepedic mattress. The real problem for me is that we live on the sixth floor and while there are stairs, the easiest and fastest way to get to the ground floor and on to the beach (which is just a few steps from the front door) is to take an elevator. Why is this a problem? I am only a dog and I have to adjust my toilet habits to allow for the time it takes to get to the elevator, through the front door, and then run to the grass alongside the shell road in front of the apartment. I am happy to say that after a few close calls, I made it to my spot every time.

Letters from Angel

I have heard that there are thirty-five other families

who live in the building called Fisherman's Haven.

I am the first dog that was ever allowed to stay in, or

even visit, one of the apartments. Mr. Levin had to

get me special training and asked the other families
if it was OK for me to stay. I am happy and grateful
that they agreed to let me live there. Mike, who is in
charge of keeping everything nice, was not so happy
to have me around for a while, but we are now best
friends. I had no trouble making friends with Mike's
wife, Vickie, who is also in charge of many things
that need to be done. You see, I make friends much
easier with women.

For walks in Florida, my regular plan is to leave
the building with either you or Mr. Levin and go
to the left down the shell road, really made of dirt

and crushed shells, which is flanked by very nice, large houses. On the side of the road facing the gulf, there are dunes that rise up above the beach to protect against any water that might come from the high tides. (I have never seen it but Mr. Levin says that when the gulf gets angry it has crossed the shell road.) Anyhow, it is a very nice walk and I take this trip on a leash almost every day. I stay on the leash because by personal experience I have found that with so many attractive smells, I am likely to disappear into the brush around the houses, never to be found again. This is an outcome that I would not like.

Letters from Angel

My favorite part of the walk is to leave the shell road and cross over to a small path that leads to Palmer Point and a park where the gulf and the Inland Waterway are just barely separated by a few feet of sand. I love to swim in the shallow part on the quiet side with the water just covering my body, my head sticking out. This is truly a restorative experience for a golden retriever. Since the weather is usually pleasant, even during the winter, and at a temperature I like, either you or Mr. Levin will take me there almost every clear day. On the way home, we usually cross over the dunes to the beach and trot back to the apartment with the incoming tide washing over my feet.

Letters from Angel

This brings me to the long story of how I met Andrea, a nice lady, and Winnie, her little gray and black shih tzu mix, who live down the shell road. Trotting home one day, I hear a dog barking incessantly. I see a blur of fur whizzing around my feet, and this tiny ball of fire jumps rapidly up to Mr. Levin, hardly able to reach his kneecap but continuing to bark. Behind the dog is a charming lady trying desperately to restore order. Finally, the lady, Andrea, reaches down and scoops up Winnie, the blur, and the barking stops momentarily. Then, Andrea invites us to come over to her house just across the dunes and drops Winnie to the ground in front of the house. At this point, Winnie conducts a head-to-tail investigation of me; she is so small I feel her under my body. I feel Mr. Levin take off my leash, I guess to keep from getting it tangled. I say to myself, "Who is this creature?" and I try to catch her as she runs around in wide circles. It is a long time since I have run this hard but as I chase her, she stops and lets me smell her. I want to show her that I love small dogs and that I would like to know her better. I have a small noise I make that humans often cannot hear that lets another dog know that we are friends. Winnie apparently heard it and she stopped, looked at me and tried to reach my lips. How tender.

Letters from Angel

Letters from Angel

This year, Winnie, Andrea, and her friend R. J., came to stay with me in Rye for ten days when you and Mr. Levin were in Germany. We had the very best time ever. I showed her all my special places to snooze, we shared food and water, walked together, played together; we had a ball. We have been close friends ever since we met and she will be my friend forever.

Family is very important

Over the years, I became accustomed to Rye and then Sarasota. Of the two, Rye was the most exciting because there was always something going on. Walks with you and Mr. Levin, shopping with you, picking up

Mr. Levin at the train. I was so glad to get to my bed

at seven and rest for the night. I even got used to you

and Mr. Levin leaving me alone to go to New York for

the theater. I felt very much in charge while you were

gone, checking to see if anything strange was going on outside. I would take a long nap and then when you came home I was at the door to greet you—and be taken outside for my pee. You always brought me home a treat. Eating leftover steak from a Broadway restaurant at midnight, can you imagine? (I sometimes joke, "What, no champagne?")

But family is the most important thing, wherever I am. I am proud of the fact that I have a chow father. I think it makes me more interesting. It is the same with most families. The mixtures make them interesting. I heard Mr. Levin say once that there were twenty-one people in his family. You have a smaller family but they are no less interesting. Between Sarasota and Rye, I think I have met them all. I was even invited over for dinner to the home of Mr. Levin's son, Jeremy, the film writer and director, and his wife, Roberta. I did not enjoy the long ride to get there so I slept a lot. However, I enjoyed the dinner. The leftover food was great. Roberta is a good cook.

Mr. Levin's daughter, Wendy, is caring and fun to play with. Like Mr. Levin she always walks me with treats in her pocket. Gordon, her husband, can fix anything. They are also great caretakers and walkers. It was fortunate that they were visiting when Mr. Levin had a terrible accident. We were walking when I saw a black lab across the road—you know how they get to me—and I went after the lab. Our leashes got tangled and Mr. Levin crashed to the pavement, hitting his head very hard. Blood started pouring from his head . . . a lot of blood. He got up, took my leash, and walked home groggily. When Wendy and Gordon saw him, they rushed him to the hospital where doctors patched him up. I was very scared for Mr. Levin but he came home from the hospital smiling and then sat down to explain to me that it was not my fault. To show that he was better, he took Gordon out for dinner that night. Twisted leashes were never a problem again. I know that if Mr. Levin drops the leash, I am to stay so he can move aside.

Hugh, his other son, who is an art-book publisher among other things, now lives in a place called La Jolla far away and comes to visit with his wife, Cynthia. It is always exciting when they come. Cynthia loves dogs and we have a special connection. Hugh always has ideas about many things that would make my life comfortable.

Many of Mr. Levin's grandchildren come as well. Julie comes with her husband, Rob. They have a darling little boy, Jonah, who is about one and a half years old, and a dog, Chloe, a small shih tzu. I am really sorry but I could not make a connection with Chloe. I love small dogs and she is only about fifteen pounds, and is cute and smart. She will not play with me or even share my food as other dogs do; I really do not know what I did, but I apologize nonetheless. I do get along fine with Jonah. He is smart even for a small baby. Even if I say this myself, I am really great with small children.

There is one caveat to the previous statement about my getting along with small children. Evan, Wendy's son, and Mireille, Evan's wife, an occupational therapist working with children, visited every Sunday afternoon when they lived nearby. (They now live in Raleigh—far away.) I looked forward to their Sunday visits. Their son, Alexander (Xander) is a smiling, laughing, lovable child. He would run his warm little hand across my back and giggle, and I would stand there and let him do this because it felt good and it made him happy. His older sister, Lyla, is about five years old. I tried everything I could think of to make friends with her but nothing worked. She is so shy. I try to send her the message that I love her and I am ready to play, but I am never able to reach her. I know she is shy because, in truth, I am shy too. I do not jump up on people and show my emotions as some other dogs do. Often, I just wait for the other person or dog to make the first move; when it does not come, I move off into a corner and try to hide.

While it is unfair to make comparisons, Jennifer, her oldest daughter, and her husband, Jamie, are real dog people. I say this even though they have two labs. Also, they have two sons, Ben and Mathew, who are great kids. All of them are always wonderful with me and know exactly how to show me their love. Mr. Levin likes them too, even though they are Boston Red Sox fans.

Letters from Angel

I see plenty of your family as well. Your two daughters, Nazare and Ariel, both love dogs—but only small dogs. Ariel is also very big on fish, and strange animals like hedgehogs. She is a teacher and loves teaching children, and I have heard her students love her as well. I do not see her as often as I see Nazare, who is a super mom and dog lover, her husband, Matt, and their almost-two-year-old Bela, who will soon have a brother. Bela and I are great friends. When she comes for a visit, her first words are, "Where is Angel?" She has a little trouble with pronunciation, but I know she is calling.

Letters from Angel

You may not believe this, but I did leave some of the
family out. I have not mentioned Zoe, Mark, and
Ezra, who live in Seattle. Or Josh, Zach, Stephanie,
and Earl who live in the Boston area and who
are great dog people, so thoughtful and kind. Or
John, who is in Los Angeles, or Rebecca and young
Cameron, who live in Raleigh. There are stories that
go along with all of them. When I joined this family, I
became one of them. I was welcomed and loved and
I want to tell everyone I know that I am grateful for
this. Some experts talk about dogs as pack animals.
I believe that this is true. But it is difficult these
days to find a pack of dogs to join, unless you go to

Alaska, and I am not about to do that. When I see all the people I have met in these two families I feel reassured—this is my pack and I love being a part of it. As for who the leader is, I will leave this decision up to you.

New York, New York,
a helluva town

The Bronx is up,
but the Battery's down

The people ride in a
hole in the ground

New York, New York,
a helluva town

{ **On the Town** }

Letters from Angel

New York, New York—a wonderful town?

As though two apartments in Sarasota were not enough, I have also stayed in two apartments in New York City: one owned by Mr. Levin's son, Hugh, and most recently in one that Mr. Levin bought to give himself yet another place to stay. I really do not remember much about Hugh's apartment except that it looked directly over Central Park, that huge oasis in the middle of the city, so big that that you can take horse-cart rides there lasting over an hour. One day Mr. Levin and I spent three hours walking and then sitting, with me smelling, meeting, and greeting scores of dogs. I had a great time mostly because I met other goldens, as well as lots of very spiffy dogs that I did not recognize, and cute, small dogs that I like. It was so exciting that we lost track of time and grew hungry. Not a problem, because there were men with carts that sell things to eat. Mr. Levin, who loves hot dogs, bought one for himself and one for me. When the man who sold them saw us sitting side by side eating hot dogs, he laughed. I guess to him, the situation was funny; to me, it was normal. I usually eat what you and Mr. Levin eat, even though some people think this is a bad idea.

Letters from Angel

Letters from Angel

Once we had our lunch, Mr. Levin thought I would enjoy a visit to the Central Park Zoo. The guards at the gate didn't like the idea, but Mr. Levin is a lawyer and advised them that since I am a service dog, under the Americans with Disabilities Act, they must let me in— so they did. I really enjoy walking around interesting places where there are lot of new smells—and for this reason the zoo was a treat for me. I especially loved the penguins. They were really cute. While we were looking at them, a man with a lot of stripes on his sleeve came over to us, patted me, and suggested to Mr. Levin that it would not be a good idea to stay much longer. He said that while I was beautiful (a

sentiment I endorsed) some of the animals might get

upset, especially if I started to bark. I had no intention

to disturb anyone, but since there were a lot of people

stopping to see what was going on, it was probably a

good idea for us to leave. In addition, we were getting tired. It had been a long day.

We were now quite far from Hugh's apartment. I could see Mr. Levin puffing a little and I really did not feel good about another long walk. Then Mr. Levin realized there was an easier way to get home. He walked me over to a stand where people with rickshaws were gathered. I really did not know anything about this but Mr. Levin explained that rickshaws were invented in China and are a regular method of transportation there. In New York City they are called Pedicabs. Some very smart man got the idea that he could make money with one in

Central Park. So Mr. Levin worked out a price with

a driver who I imagine thought it would be great

fun to pull a man and a dog through heavy traffic

with taxi cabs sliding in and out of lanes along with

horse-drawn carriages full of people also trying to

get through the crowded street. Well, it was not that

much fun. It was OK for Mr. Levin, but I struggled.

First, it was a challenge to get all eighty-one pounds

of me on the cart. The driver tried to lift me onto the

seat beside Mr. Levin but he could not do it, so he

put me on the step by Mr. Levin's feet. I was scared to

death; it was shaky. I did not realize that it was a long

way to the apartment and mostly uphill. Also, that cab

drivers have no manners. They do not stay in their

lanes, they cut in front of you, and they honk their

horns. In addition, everyone was looking at us—a

dog squeezed on the step of a rickshaw and an older

man being pulled through traffic. I am grateful to the saints who watch over dogs for getting us back to Hugh's apartment.

When Hugh moved out of his apartment, I thought my days in midtown Manhattan were over. I could handle the apartment in Sarasota but my favorite spot of all is what Mr. Levin calls "the biggest doghouse in the world" in Rye, with the lawns right outside so that I can pee on them when I am ready. But as fate would have it, Mr. Levin and Hugh found another apartment very close to Central Park on the eleventh floor of a big building. I wished they had consulted me when they did this. The reason for getting this apartment, located at Fifty-sixth Street and Sixth Avenue, was so Hugh, Cynthia, Paula, and other members of the family could use it. It was also important to Mr. Levin since he often travels from Sarasota to New York and his office is nearby. He could stay in the city and not have to take the train home. I hoped it would not too bad for me, either, since it was still close to Central Park, which I love. You and Mr. Levin took turns walking me and I enjoy your company. The real problem is leaving the apartment, which entails going down a long hallway, waiting for the elevator to come, descending eleven floors in a service elevator (I was too big to fit in the regular elevators, they said) and then heading out to the street. Getting over to Central Park takes more time and can be a real problem especially if you have to pee, bad. Sometimes I just made it out the sliding front door of the apartment. In addition, there are lots of dogs living in the building. I am not there often enough to get to know them, but walking down the hallway to the elevator I smell where they made their marks on the carpet. When I added my mark, you and Mr. Levin were unhappy with me. Walking in our neighborhood in New York is very dangerous. To get to our apartment from Central

Letters from Angel

Park, we must cross Fifty-seventh Street at Sixth Avenue, a very busy intersection. One day walking home with Mr. Levin, we stopped obediently at the curb on Fifty-seventh Street to allow buses and a long line of taxis and cars to go by. When the light changed to show it was safe to cross, we started out, but when we reached the middle of Fifty-seventh Street, I had a sudden urge to pee and crouched down to relieve myself. When I looked up, I saw cars turning from Sixth Avenue heading right for me. I heard the traffic cop whistling frantically, a squealing of car breaks, saw Mr. Levin standing in front of me waving his arms. It was a scary situation but once I

start peeing with a full bladder, I cannot stop. When I was finished, I walked on nonchalantly. As we got to the other side of the street, I heard some unpleasant words from the cab drivers passing by and a very menacing look from the cop as he untangled this mess. However,

Letters from Angel

I promise unlimited loyalty and devotion to the people I live with. I would never be critical of anything they do. If they like apartments, even in Manhattan, I am with them.

Complaint department

I rarely, if ever, gripe about anything, but I must say there should be a law against fireworks. There are fireworks at Playland, the amusement park, in Rye. While we are located about three to four miles from there, they have fireworks twice a week and I can see and hear them. They are bright and loud, and I cannot handle them. As soon as the vibrations go through the air, I pick them up, and start to shiver and shake. I go from room to room seeking a place to hide. Once when Mr. Levin was watching me, he tried everything to make me comfortable. He is not as cool as you, so he took me outside hoping that if I looked at the pretty designs in the sky, I would quiet down. This did not work. Another time he put me in his car and took me to the movies hoping that staying in a dark area would distract me. This didn't work either. The music playing throughout the picture went *boom boom boom.* It was worse than the fireworks. They looked at him funny when he took me into the movie theater, and when he took me out the ticket taker, a real smarty, said, "Didn't your dog like the movie?"

I also do not like the sound of thunder. I am not sure why many times when it rains there is thunder, before, during, and after the storm. This is as bad as fireworks, maybe worse. I shake at thunder even more than fireworks and I do the same things. I run and hide. Mr. Levin, who always seems to get stuck with me on firework and thunder nights, does not have a clue as to how to stop me from shaking. One night, during a bad storm, I ran downstairs and went into the garage. Mr. Levin thought I wanted to take a ride, so he

opened the back door of the car and started to drive

me around Rye. The rain was pelting down and it was

stuffy in the car. I made a little noise, a sort of half

bark, and Mr. Levin thought I wanted him, as usual, to

put the back window down. He lowered the window

just as a huge rain cloud broke all over the car and a gust of wind drove the rain to the front seat all over Mr. Levin. He was not a happy camper.

Again, I am generally not a complainer. I walk in the rain without an umbrella. I do not need a dog sweater even when it is cold. However, there must be a way to stop the fireworks and the thunder. My brain is only one-third the size of a human brain. I do the best I can with what I have and I depend on people like you and Mr. Levin to fix these little things. Isn't that fair?

Letters from Angel

The Angel "diet"

When I came to stay at your house I weighed fifty-seven pounds. My first meal there was dog food that the shelter provided; I was famished, so I ate it. It obviously left you with the misconception that I would eat dog food, so you brought home a variety of brands from the supermarket. The first morning I thought I made it clear that this was not acceptable by not eating the food you put in my plate. Then, meal after meal, I decided to let you know that my palate was more sophisticated by either not eating or just eating a little bit. After demonstrating that I was not interested in dog food, I came to the table as you were finishing a meal and looked at you and Mr. Levin with my big brown eyes. This was a crucial point in our relationship. Had you denied me any table food, I would have finally eaten the dog food. But you blinked, and gave me some of the rotisserie chicken you were eating. I enjoyed this and to show you I did, I rubbed your legs to let you know that I was not a fan of dog food.

Since you have a passion for cooking, you decided to make my meals personally. I love the hamburgers that you made, the hot dogs, and especially the lamb shanks. I adore lamb shanks because you cut the meat off and then I would have the bone to chew on for days. As far as I can remember, there were always partially eaten lamb shanks on the kitchen floor for weeks so that in between meals I could use them for a snack. It got to the point that I would sniff at your grocery bag when you came home to see if you had bought a rotisserie chicken for me. I like my chicken warm and it is best when you have just returned from the supermarket. I have two all-time favorites: lamb chops and steak. I like the meat done medium, not too rare. Bones are also important, especially with the steak. The T-bones in the sirloin steaks are very tasty.

Letters from Angel

I always loved it when you and Mr. Levin went out
to dinner. To show that you appreciated my being
good while you were gone, you always brought me
some treat in a doggy bag. Except for the Chinese
one, I love your choice in restaurants. My favorite
was when you brought home short ribs with the
bone. I enjoyed the cheese pizza, and the veal chops
were also very good, as were the flounder and baked
salmon. I think that when you order your dinner
at a restaurant, you choose your meal with me in
mind. There was a time when you introduced me
to cheeses and cold cuts so you could wrap the bad
tasting medicines in them. I was very fond of lox,

corned beef, ham, and good Swiss cheese, and these delicacies helped me when I needed it.

I hear many of your friends say "you are spoiling this dog" and I really resent this. Everyone needs good food. If they were given special dog foods like Science Diet, they would never eat. They might be healthy, but they would not be happy. I should make one confession. After a steady diet of all those human foods, once in a while I really enjoy a can of Mighty Dog, especially the lamb and rice combination. Your friends and family said that my gaining weight from fifty-seven pounds to ninety-one

pounds was bad for me. But when I started to lose weight and lost over ten pounds, that was not such a good idea either. Personally, I think I look better when my body is filled out. No one ever said I was not a pretty dog because I was a little heavier than I should be. So there.

Sometimes imagination makes things
far worse than they are;
yet without imagination
not much can be done.

Those people who are imaginative can see
many more dangers than perhaps exist;

But for everyone . . . this one lesson:
never give in, never give in, never, never.

{ **Sir Winston Churchill** }

Letters from Angel

The crisis

When we are in Rye, you usually take one long
weekend every three weeks or so to visit your family
in Sarasota. Upon leaving, you kiss me as though
you will never come back, because you do not like
flying in an airplane (I know how you feel). I sort of
look forward to being alone with Mr. Levin. He likes
to walk but I cannot go as fast with him as I do with
you. He thinks that to keep me from being bored he
has to take me to special places. So, he takes me to
the town park and the boardwalk where I can meet
other dogs and find new smells. He also takes me
on one of my favorite walks down a hidden path,

over the rocks, and back to the hidden pool of water from Playland Lake. On the road in front of the Rye house toward the mill pond, there is a small opening to the left. Looking carefully, there is a narrow path overgrown with strange plants and, be warned, poison ivy, which Mr. Levin always touches with his feet, to his sorrow. The path looks impassable because there are large broken tree branches stretched across it. However, those nimble as I am can step over the branches and follow the path to Playland Lake, reachable only after climbing a series of large rocks. Can you imagine how exciting this is for me? When I get to the rocks, I climb up, stretch my neck so I can see all around the lake, stand there erect, and rest. Then Mr. Levin usually gives me a treat, to encourage me to start down the rocks in the direction of a smaller pond.

You always tell Mr. Levin not to take me there because you are afraid he will fall on the rocks and break his hip, which would be a sad thing to happen to a ninety-two-year-old man. However, for your information, Mr. Levin has never fallen, not once. I make sure of that because I stretch out the leash until it is tight to give him extra support. (As an aside, while we are discussing this, you did fall, not here, but at another place where I swim, slipping on the rocks and breaking your wrist. I was very sorry about this, but happy you got better quickly.)

The small pond has a rock bottom. I step into the water and Mr. Levin holds on to my leash so I can go swimming. It is very refreshing and I feel like I am just a puppy. After the swimming, I am very frisky walking back to the road. We cross the road and continue the walk through a marina filled with boats of all sizes, then head for home through a small stand of trees where rabbits and the groundhog live. So it is no wonder, with all these diversions, I like to stay with Mr. Levin. Also, I am serving a purpose for him. The reason he adopted me was that Mr. Levin's wife of sixty-eight years died and the doctor treating his sadness told him to get a dog. I was the lucky one.

After a very exciting day and a good meal made by Mr. Levin just for me, I went to bed. When you are away I still sleep in your room. I miss you but I have all your smells there so this makes the separation easier. I try to keep an eye on Mr. Levin but he is a heavy sleeper and does not even know I look in on him from time to time. On this fateful night, all was quiet until I felt that I had to poop, badly. I went to

Letters from Angel

Mr. Levin's bedroom and made my little noise that says I need help. He did not hear me. Since it was urgent I went down the stairs to go out to the back lawn. During the day that door is open so I can go out. I did not remember it is closed at night. I tried to move it but it was locked. I ran up and down, slipped on the hardwood floors, and pooped. I tried to get up, but I found I could not move. Nothing. My legs were splayed and I was stuck. I do not know how long I stayed there, but early in the morning I heard Mr. Levin looking for me. When he found me on the floor with the poop around me, I was devastated. I try so hard to please you and Mr. Levin

and here I was unable to move with poop all over
the floor. Mr. Levin is a kind man. He patted me
and said that I should not worry. He cleaned up
the poop and tried to lift me so I could walk. I tried
my best to get up but I could not move. He could
not move me as I am an eighty-one-pound dog,
too heavy for him to lift. He patted me again, gave
me some water, and then I heard his car leave the
garage. I knew he was going for help.

In a very short time, Mr. Levin was back with two
men and they rolled me on a blanket, picked me up,
and carried me to the car. They put me on the back

seat and rode with us to my regular vet. They carried
me inside and put me on the floor. In a few minutes,
the vet was there and bent down to examine me.
After a lot of looking and poking, the vet said I was
OK but Mr. Levin had to leave me there overnight in
his hospital so he could give me some steroid shots
that would make me better. Mr. Levin left to take the
men who helped him home but told me he would
be back.

I was a hungry, thirsty, and very unhappy dog. The
vet arranged for some water but it was hard for
me to drink spread out flat on the floor. Just the

day before I had been playing with Mr. Levin and

looking forward to another day of fun before you

came back. Now I had disgraced myself, could

not walk, and was lying on a cold floor in a dog hospital. I now know, but did not know then, that after Mr. Levin took his helpers home, he called you in Sarasota, and you were coming back as soon as you could get a flight. Mr. Levin came back in the afternoon. He was very sad. He loved me so much and he was worried. He asked the vet who would be staying with me during the night. The vet said that his staff went home at seven o'clock and the security guard would be there with me if I needed help. I had never seen Mr. Levin *really* angry. He told the vet this was not satisfactory and that he was taking me home NOW! The vet tried to explain but Mr. Levin

Letters from Angel

was not listening. He turned to one of the staff, a

very nice young man, and said, "Give me a hand

and we will bring Angel to my car." The young man

was puzzled but when the vet said it was OK he got a towel which he put around my belly and lifted me up. I stood! Yes, I was wobbly and weak, but I could move and I walked one short step at a time. When we reached Mr. Levin's car, I was lifted gently into the back seat. I was dazed but thrilled more than you can ever imagine to be going home.

However, the adventure was still not over. I was lying on the back seat not knowing if I could really walk on my own. I certainly could not hope to jump out of the back seat as I normally do. As we pulled into the driveway, by some divine providence, our friend Barry was there with his dog. When Mr. Levin explained what had happened, Barry told Mr. Levin to bring my bed downstairs where I could go outside if needed, then turned his dog over to Mr. Levin, reached into the back seat, patted me gently, moved me to him, lifted me into his arms, and deposited me right on my Posturepedic bed. I was so grateful to everyone. I knew you would be home soon and you would get me better.

Paula to the rescue

You returned that night and we had our usual girl talk. You told me how sorry you were, that I was a good girl, and you loved me. You grasped me around the stomach and got me up on my feet, helping me to walk outside to pee. I was still very shaky, and slipping on the polished floors. The vet had sent home medicine so you gave this to me and it made me feel a little better. You had seen an ad for a harness with two grips, one at the shoulders and another at the hips. When you saw that I was slipping, you knew I would need this and had it sent by overnight courier service. Little by little over the next few days with the help of the steroids, I began to walk again. The medicine slowed me down so I was no longer an old dog with the vigor of a puppy, but I was coming back.

In the meantime, Mr. Levin was out buying almost everything in sight that might help. He blamed himself for not getting up to let me out. If he had done so, he said, we could have avoided all of this, and I would be the old happy dog I was the day before this happened. The first things he bought were a two-by-four piece of plywood and a dolly. He was going to construct a device on which to pull me around if I could not walk. Since I started to walk, it never got used, and is now stored in the garage right next to the crate and the collar for the invisible fence. Nevertheless, he made some very good purchases. There are thirteen steps from the first floor to the second floor. They are polished and since he was afraid I would slip going up and down the steps, he bought, and you installed, non-skid treads. He also bought throw rugs to cover every polished floor. After the new harness came with all these adaptations, I was better but really not as good as I wished.

You and Mr. Levin decided that we would change vets and found a wonderful place close by. The vet was nice. He examined me carefully and asked you

lots of questions. At the end he said that he felt I
should have some tests and made an appointment
for me to have X-rays and an MRI. I had no idea
what he was talking about but apparently you and
Mr. Levin did. You did not look happy but in a few
days we took a long ride to a special place where
they have dog doctors and machines for everything.
I spent a full day there and at the end I met a very
nice vet. He did not seem very happy with what
he found. But I came back home and back to our
routine. What was different was that it was hard
for me to stand. I heard you and Mr. Levin say that
they could not give me the good medicine for my

back because it is a medicine you cannot give with steroids. Sometimes, you had to pick me up with the back handle of the harness. With the rugs down, I felt very steady unless I wandered off and got on to a shiny floor. I think the steroids hopped me up so I walked around and around. After a while, I would get tired and then sit down. I was really worried. Also, I seemed always to be pulling to the right and I would find my head leaning against the wall or cabinets. The worst part of this was that I could not control my peeing and pooping. You would take me out into the yard every two hours during the day and several times at night. It worked sometimes but other times I could not control it and pooped or peed wherever I was. For a proud lady, this was devastating. It took all my courage not to cry. I lived for the good days, and I was happy to see you smiling like you used to.

One of the most interesting things about living in Rye is that there are many different animals around. The deer come most afternoons and evenings. They have found good food on our property. Several years ago they kept coming until they ate all 300 tulip plants you had planted. There are lots of squirrels and chipmunks. And there are lots and lots of ducks

that come every morning because you feed them
and put out water for them. I am really not very fond
of ducks, so when I am in the yard and I see them,
I give them my most menacing look and they leave.
One day, I tasted the water that you put out for them
in a big yellow flat pan. It was delicious, better than
any water I get, even with ice cubes. So since the

steroids make me thirsty,
when I am out in the
yard I go for the water
in the yellow flat pan. If
it is empty, you will fill it
up for me. I do not know
what makes it so tasty, but
it's a treat.

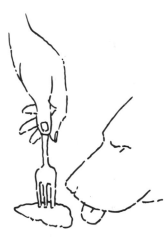

You and Mr. Levin tried to keep everything as
normal as you could. We walked our same walks.
You cooked food for me that you knew I liked. My
favorite was barbecued chicken and rice. And if you

had steak, you would cut up some pieces for me. We had visitors who came and sat in the new family room that looks like a glass house built in the trees, and they made a big fuss over me. Every once in a while you would take my harness off so I could feel like a pretty young girl.

An adventure to remember

As you know, I love the water. All goldens do. I live by the water in Rye. Mr. Levin often takes me to walk on the dock that is anchored to posts on the lawn. From the dock I look at the twelve feet of rocks that are exposed at low tide and I have always dreamt

about climbing down the rocks and swimming in the

Long Island Sound. Each time I walk by these rocks,

I try to start down but neither you or Mr. Levin will

let me. I am not very good with calendars but I have

been told that the following adventure took place

on a dark night on October 2, 2010. Despite all my problems, I was feeling pretty good. I had just had a shot of steroids. This makes me thirsty, which makes me drink and pee. I signaled to you that I needed to go out on the lawn and you opened the door. I went out, had my pee, and looked around. No Paula. So I figured this was my big chance. I went for the shore and I could feel my feet hit the wet rocks. I was on a smooth ride down, even with my harness on. I never felt better in my life. It was so dark I could not see anything but I could feel the mud under my feet and the water. Now for a nice swim. Just then I saw a flashlight searching the rocks and your voice calling

Letters from Angel

"Angel! Angel!!" In a minute, I could see you in
your night clothes coming down the rocks shining
the flashlight at me. I started to swim and just as I
was ready to pull away, I felt you grabbing my back
harness. I tried to swim away but you were too strong
for me. You slowly pulled me back and then, I am

not sure how, dragged me up the rocks to the lawn. I was very muddy, but you were a soggy mess. I added to this by shaking all the muddy water on me all over you. You are a determined lady and you got me back into a bathtub filled with soapy water and cleaned me up. As I dried off, you got in the shower and washed away all the gunk. Then you brushed me, took me to my mattress, and turned me on my side, without the harness, to dream wonderful dreams. This did wonders for my morale at a time when I needed a boost.

Somewhere over the rainbow
Way up high,
There's a land that I heard of
Once in a lullaby.

Somewhere over the rainbow
Skies are blue,
And the dreams that you
dare to dream
Really do come true.

{ *"Over the Rainbow"* }
—*E. Y. Harburg*

Letters from Angel

The return to Sarasota

You and Mr. Levin went to Germany, where Mr. Levin had business and Andrea, who lives down the road from us in Sarasota, her dog, Winnie, whom I love, and Andrea's friend R. J., came to Rye to stay with me. I just loved this. First because Winnie, even though she is tiny and just a little over a year old, is my best friend. She is so perky that she keeps me happy and playful. Also, she has someone who writes letters to me and signs her name, making believe Winnie wrote it. I know Winnie cannot write! Andrea and R. J. are good with dogs. They are stricter than you and Mr. Levin but I can handle this because they are both so loving.

Letters from Angel

Nevertheless, while it was a good break, I was glad to see you and Mr. Levin back home.

The days were getting shorter and the weather colder. It was time for us to move back to Sarasota for the winter. Andrea suggested that instead of flying back to Florida, they would rent a car and drive Winnie and me down. I thought this was a dandy idea and when they put a rug down in the back of their big Ford Explorer and Winnie and I got inside, I was so happy. Winnie and I slept side by side all night with a few stops for peeing. I missed you but you flew down the next day and in a few hours I was back in Sarasota.

Letters from Angel

The days in Sarasota are always great. I love the walks. I love to swim in the gulf. You are a great sport. You get into those sexy purple bathing suits and swim right along with me. Mike and Vickie, who take care of the apartments, are so nice. Even though they initially made it very hard for me to stay here, everyone makes a big fuss over me. There is a very nice vet in Sarasota, Dr. Calloway. She and you would work over my medicines, trying things to make me better. I think I heard you talking the last time I was there about a check up for my level of pain. I do have lots of pain, especially in the area of my back legs. You have been giving me pain pills that help but is it is so discouraging not to be able to walk to Palmer Point anymore or hop into the back of the car without you holding my rear up. For a proud, loving dog this is very discouraging.

Day of woe, years of peace

During the last few days, things have gotten much worse. Mr. Levin took me for a walk and I could not walk more than a few steps. You would try to cheer me with love, but I just looked at you with my big brown eyes. I know you could see the pain I was suffering. The steroids were not working. I needed more pain pills. I had a good idea as to what was coming but I really did not want to show it. You and

Mr. Levin took me to see Andrea and Winnie. When

Winnie came out, she danced around me—and

you know what, I danced right along, full of pain,

though I was not going to show it. That night, you

cooked me a small steak because you knew this was

my favorite food. It was really delicious. The next

morning we were all up early for a walk on the

beach. It was so beautiful. What a lovely thing to

remember.

We drove to the vet's office and took some pictures,

then went inside. The lady asked me, "Are you

Letters from Angel

Angel?" She knew I was and showed me into a little room with a nice soft blanket on the floor. You lay down alongside me. I could see Mr. Levin crying and he joined us kneeling down. We must have stayed

touching each other for a long time. Dr. Calloway came much too soon, but it was time. She told us that she would like me to look at you and Mr. Levin. She would give me some medicine and I would go to sleep. I felt a little prick in my leg, then a warm feeling all over. My eyes closed. No pain. Thank you, Paula. Thank you, Mr. Levin.

Letters from Angel

Postscript

When we adopted Angel, neither Paula nor I considered the possibility of Angel's death. At that time I was seeking comfort for the loss of my wife, Marcia, my companion for sixty-eight years. Even though Angel's coat was caked with mud, when she looked at us through the bars of her cage at the adoption center, we bonded. We knew Angel was a senior dog, but we never considered how at some point in the not-too-distant future we might lose her. Most experts believe that our experience is universal, that bonding between human and dog takes place involuntarily and without conscious thought.

Letters from Angel

We spent five wonderful years with Angel. Then, in one night, the world changed for Angel and for us. She was unable to rise or walk. However, with medication and a new harness she fought her way back. We were able to adjust her to the new circumstances, and for a while it appeared that she was comfortable to live within her limitations. We were alerted by doctors, and eventually came to accept that there might come a time when Angel would not be able to continue on, even with medication. She had two tumors, one in her brain.

When we asked the vet for guidance, she said, "When it is time, Angel will let you know." A few weeks later, when Angel was walking down the shell road in our vacation home in Sarasota attempting to play with her best friend, Winnie, Angel sat down and looked up at Paula in pain. There was no mistaking the look in those shining eyes. They were saying, "This is the time."

We had no concept of what our experience would be like in deciding to end the life of a dog we loved so much. Paula and I talked over all the options available to us until finally we were able to summon the courage to call Dr. Calloway and set a date to have Angel put down and cremated. We cherished our last evening with Angel, who seemed to brighten for a bit while enjoying her favorite dinner of steak. She slept in bed for the last night, took her last walk in the morning, gathered all her energy to climb into the back seat of the car for the last time, and with her head jutting out the window, sniffed the autumn air as usual.

Paula, Angel, and I walked into Dr. Calloway's office and waited to be called. A few minutes later the door opened to the examination room and Angel walked in. Normally, Angel would get "freaked out" when she saw a white doctor's jacket, but on this day she slid to the floor and into her favorite resting position— one front paw crossed over the other. Dr. Calloway explained the procedure to us. She and her assistant would be with Angel on the floor. Her assistant would hold Angel and put a slight amount of pressure on the vein of the front leg and Dr. Calloway would administer the euthanasia solution.

Both Paula and I knelt to the floor holding Angel as Dr. Calloway inserted the fine needle. Angel looked up at us for a moment, then slowly closed her eyes and lay there peacefully. She took a deep breath and in about ten seconds appeared to drift off to sleep. A few breaths followed and then Angel was at peace. Dr. Calloway left the room so that we could be alone with Angel. We held her for the last time as tears streamed down our faces.

Letters from Angel

The first night without Angel was difficult. Paula put Angel's bed in a guest bedroom and packed her leash and other belongings. It was too early to talk about whether or not we would look for another dog. It was November 13, and there was to be no further conversation through to the end of the year. Both Paula and I felt the loss, seeking support from each other. Angel lived on in our hearts. It was not until January that I started thinking about another dog and mustered the courage to talk to Paula about it. Paula was warming to the idea of a small dog, but I wanted to adopt another golden retriever about three to five years old.

Letters from Angel

In February, without discussing it with Paula, I managed a visit to the Humane Society in Sarasota. There I met a gorgeous three-year-old golden retriever named Calloway. Unfortunately, we were third in line and Calloway was adopted by a family with two children. However, this started us on a hunt for another golden. Month after month went by without any progress. In April, Paula spotted an advertisement for a four-month-old golden retriever puppy named Harvey. It was a golden, but a puppy? We decided to check it out and, as you might have guessed, we now have Harvey in the family. Once again there was involuntary bonding. We met Harvey and fell in love again.

Goldens are generally beautiful dogs, but Harvey is a show-stopper. At full size he is expected to weigh ninety pounds. We are now going down the checklist: toilet training (done), obedience school (done), no jumping (in progress), staying within limits (in process). On the positive side, while golden puppies are high octane, they are also loving and mellow. Harvey takes regular naps and sleeps through the night and can be left alone without testing out his new teeth on shoes or other household objects.

I thought I would share this postscript for other owners who have experienced the heartbreak of putting a dog to sleep. Angel lived for her full fifteen years, but regrettably only five with us. She still lives on in our hearts and mind. With Harvey as a part of the family we are now privileged to be a part of shaping a new life while further enriching our own.

Letters from Angel

Acknowledgments

This book was difficult to write because it was created immediately after Angel died. I was helped by the support of my assistant, Paula Drost. Her recollections of Angel were crucial. I am also grateful to Mark Weinstein, senior editor at Skyhorse, for his encouragement, counsel, and keen observation.

While all the words are mine (and I take full responsibility for them), the creative contributions from designer Keira McGuinness and illustrator Mark Parker made assembled words into a book. Keira's talent transformed the text so that it reaches out and connects to the reader. Keira also did this for my previous book, and hopefully will join me in my next one.

Mark Parker was introduced to me by his former associate, Rob Bloom, a talent on his own. This is Mark's first published book. He is a graduate of the Tyler School of Art at Temple University. Using the extraordinary photographs taken by Tiffany Schwarz (who somehow became Angel's official photographer), Mark was able to visualize Angel, bringing her to life in forty extraordinary sketches and on the cover.

Finally, I am profoundly grateful to Tony Lyons,